CONTENTS

NODDY

ANNUAL 2008

Pedigree®

Published by Pedigree Books Limited
Beech Hill House, Walnut Gardens, Exeter, Devon EX4 4DH.
E-mail books@pedigreegroup.co.uk
Published 2007

£7.99

WELCOME TO TOYLAND

HELLO EVERYONE!

Hello, everyone! My name is Noddy and I live in my own little House-For-One in Toy Town. I'm just going to pick up the first passenger of the day in my red and yellow taxi, but I must remember not to drive too fast or I shall be in trouble with Mr Plod! I'm going to take Tessie Bear and Bumpy Dog to Toy Town Station so that they can catch the Toyland Express. Before you read all about my adventures, come with me to meet them and some of my other friends...

TESSIE BEAR AND BUMPY DOG

Tessie Bear and Bumpy Dog
Kind Tessie Bear lives in a little pink house with Bumpy Dog, the bumpiest, jumpiest dog in Toyland! She keeps chickens in her garden and uses their eggs to make delicious googleberry muffins for us all.

BIG-EARS

This cheerful gnome is my best friend and he lives in Toadstool Wood. Big-Ears is a hundred years old and very wise indeed! If ever I have a problem, he is usually nearby on his bicycle to help me solve it.

MR. PLOD

Mr Plod rides around Toy Town on his bicycle, looking out for mischief-makers. If anyone is misbehaving, he soon puts a stop to it by blowing his whistle and shouting, "Halt, in the name of Plod!"

MARTHA MONKEY

This cheeky little monkey is Toyland's practical joker and she seems to play most of her tricks on me! She loves to whizz around on her roller skates and sometimes gets told off by Mr Plod for going too fast.

MR. SPARKS

Mr Sparks runs the Toy Town garage and I often have to ask him to mend my car. If it breaks down, he will even come to the rescue with his tow truck! He can fix just about anything and likes inventing things, too.

DINAH DOLL

Dinah Doll runs the market stall in Toy Town, which sells everything you could ever need and more. Dinah is always ready for an emergency, too, as she is the town's Fire Chief and drives the fire engine.

8

MR. JUMBO

Peanut-loving Mr Jumbo is a gentle elephant who likes to paint and his best friend is little Clockwork Mouse. Everyone knows that they should get out of the way if Mr Jumbo feels a sneeze coming!

MISS PINK CAT

As the owner of Toy Town's Ice Cream Parlour, Miss Pink Cat takes great pride in her appearance and good manners. She serves the yummiest home-made ice creams and the creamiest milk shakes, too!

SLY AND GOBBO

These two naughty goblins live in a tree house in the Dark Wood. The biggest troublemakers in Toyland, they play tricks on people and often try to 'borrow' my little taxi. Luckily, they always get caught!

9

A NICE DAY OUT

A picnic is a lovely way
To spend a sunny summer's day!
We drive out to a pretty spot,
Then while the barbecue gets hot
We lay our cloth flat on the ground
And Bumpy Dog bounces around.
When he's tired, he sits and waits
As Tessie puts out all the plates.
At last it's time to drink and eat –
This picnic really is a treat!

T IS FOR
TOY TOWN

Noddy lives in Toy Town and Tessie Bear is one of his friends. Toy Town and Tessie both begin with the 't' sound. Colour in the things you can see here that also begin with the 't' sound and draw a circle round the one left over. What sound does it begin with?

NODDY AND THE FACTORY

Noddy was driving through the Toyland countryside one sunny afternoon when he saw a large sign that was sticking upright in the middle of a field. He slowed down and stopped to look at it. "Sold," he said, reading the sign out loud. Puzzled, Noddy drove on to Toy Town.

SOLD

Noddy's friends were very surprised to hear about the sign. "Who could have bought the field?" they asked each other. "And why?" Tessie Bear thought the field might be turned into a lake with boats, while Master Tubby Bear hoped a fair would go on it.

Sly and Gobbo seemed to know all about the sign already. They told everyone that a beautiful factory was going to be built on the field. "Are you sure? I have never heard of a beautiful factory," said Noddy. "Of course we're sure!" Gobbo grinned.

"We've heard," Gobbo added, "that this factory will make things like sweets and cookies and googleberry ice cream. Isn't that right, Sly?" Seeing Gobbo wink, Sly nodded enthusiastically. Noddy agreed that it would be good to have more treats.

The next time Noddy drove past, he was surprised to see that a large, ugly block had been built in the field. "That's not the beautiful factory that Sly and Gobbo talked about!" he exclaimed. He saw the goblins nearby and went over to speak to them.

"Not beautiful?" gasped Gobbo. "We think it's a fine building. I suppose we could have a word with the owners if you don't like it." Sly suggested adding some decoration. "Perhaps some round or pointy bits?" he smiled. "Squares and circles?"

When Noddy went to see the factory the next day, he was pleased to find that it looked more like the buildings in Toy Town and was almost beautiful; there were even some flowers in a window box. "That's much better," Noddy said to himself.

Noddy looked at the front entrance, with its pillars like the ones at the Town Hall. The arch above them was just like the one at Mr Sparks's garage and the clock in the middle was like the one at Toy Town Station. Noddy walked round to the back.

There were bricks of all different shapes at the back of the factory: squares, rectangles, triangles and arches. Noddy liked them, as they reminded him of his House-For-One. In fact, the more he looked, the more like his bricks they seemed.

Noddy told his friends to come and see what they thought. "I like those squares and stripes," said Mr Jumbo. "I think I may have seen them somewhere before…" Everyone agreed that the factory did look beautiful and fitted in well with the town.

Suddenly, black smoke began to pour from the factory chimney and darken the blue sky. "I thought they were making nice things like googleberry ice cream in there!" cried Martha Monkey. "Why is all this horrible smoke coming out?"

Sly and Gobbo told the crowd that ice cream machines were noisy and made lots of smoke. "They haven't guessed that we're making things from our old junk," Sly tittered that night. "We'll be rich when we sell it all!" Gobbo sniggered.

"The thing is," said Sly, "we don't know how to make the treats we promised." "That's easy," chuckled Gobbo. "We steal some from the Ice Cream Parlour and sell them with the other things." The goblins had no idea that someone was listening.

As Dinah Doll was telling Mr Plod about the goblins, her friends reported all the things that were missing from buildings in Toy Town. "A roof, a clock, some pillars...slow down, I can't keep up!" said Mr Plod, trying to make some notes.

Mr Plod went to arrest the goblins. "I know what you've been up to," he boomed. "When you've taken back all the things you stole for your so-called factory, you can give everyone googleberry ice cream to say sorry...and you'll have to pay for it!"

CIRCLE TIME

4

Toy Town is made up of all sorts of different shapes. Noddy can see lots of round things as he drives up to Mr Sparks's garage! Look carefully at the picture and see how many circles you can spot.

TOY TOWN SHAPES

Noddy has been looking at some of the other shapes in Toy Town. Count the shapes below and use a pencil to practise writing the numbers.

1 1 1 1 1   circle

2 2 2 2 2   triangle

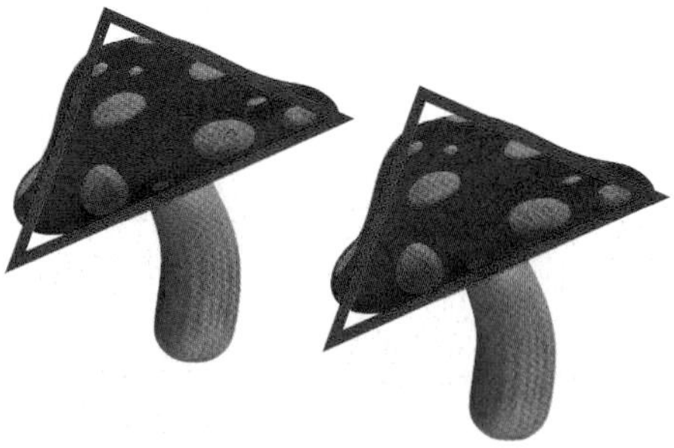

3 3 3 3 3   star

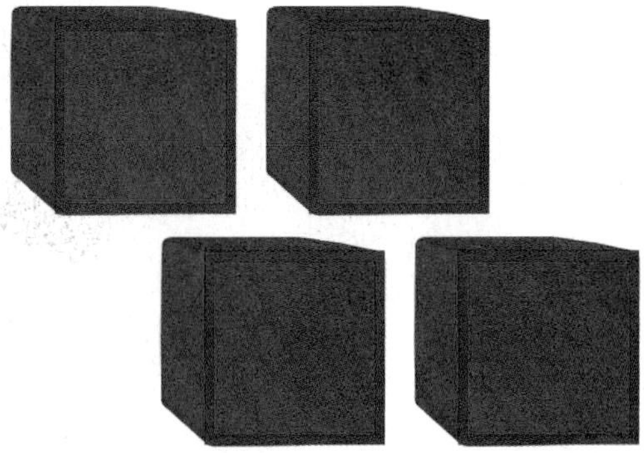

4 4 4 4 4   square

NODDY'S SHAPES

I think a circle is my favourite shape –
The shape of the moon and the sun,
Of car wheels and headlamps, biscuits and tarts,
And bricks on my nice House-For-One!

Some of my house bricks are triangles,
The shape of a boat sails at sea,
A tinkling instrument and sandcastle flags,
And the pieces of toast for my tea!

I also have bricks that are square-shaped
Next to my little front door,
They're the shape of the checks on Mr Sparks' coat,
And a hopscotch space, chalked on the floor!

TEA TIME
AT NODDY'S

Noddy has invited four of his friends for tea. Use a pencil or your finger to show Big-Ears, Master Tubby Bear, Tessie Bear and Dinah Doll which way they should go to reach Noddy's House-For-One. Watch out for the goblins, though – they're not invited!

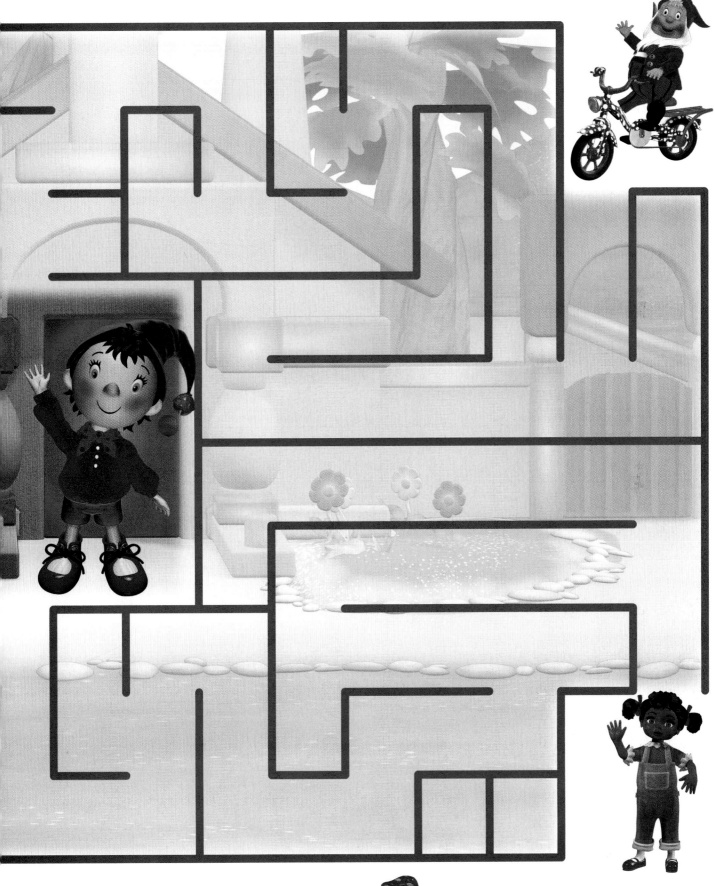

THE TOY TOWN CLOCKS

Mr Sparks was going on holiday to the seaside. As he locked up his garage, Noddy arrived to take him to the train station. "Remember to look after your car, Noddy," he said. "I shan't be here if anything goes wrong." "Yes, Mr Sparks," Noddy chuckled.

Noddy dropped Mr Sparks at Toy Town Station. "See you next week, Noddy," called Mr Sparks, as he waved from the Toyland Express. He noticed that the station clock was slow, but before he could warn Noddy, the train moved away with a hiss.

The next morning, something strange happened: the Town Hall clock chimed five o'clock, even though everyone was up and beginning their day. The townspeople gathered around the clock and looked up at it, wondering what was wrong.

"The hands must be stuck," said Dinah Doll. "Perhaps it needs winding up, like me," suggested Clockwork Mouse. "Mr Sparks has keys to all the clocks, but he's away for the week," said Noddy. "We shall have to use another clock until he comes back."

Noddy went to look at the station clock, but that was almost as slow. "My alarm clock must be right," he said. When Big-Ears checked his clock, though, it showed a different time to Noddy's. In fact, no one could agree on what the right time was!

Early the following morning, Noddy was surprised to hear a knock at the door. "Aren't you coming out to play?" asked Master Tubby Bear. "It's eleven o'clock!" "But my clock says seven o'clock," Noddy told his friends. "I'm not dressed yet!"

Noddy put his clock forward a few hours, but while he was playing a noisy game with Bumpy Dog the next morning, Mr Plod blew his whistle. "Be quiet, Noddy! You're waking everyone up!" he told him. "I thought it was nine o'clock," Noddy explained.

Noddy put his clock back again, but Miss Pink Cat came knocking at his door the next day. "You were supposed to pick me up at ten o'clock, Noddy," she said crossly, "and you're very late." "Oh, dear," sighed Noddy. "I thought it was only seven o'clock."

Noddy wanted to be on time for his passengers, but how could he when no one could agree what the right time was? To make sure he was awake when people needed him, Noddy decided to get up early and go to bed late. By the third day, he was worn out!

Noddy became so tired that he fell asleep on the station platform. "We really must find a new clock," sighed Tessie Bear. "Poor Noddy needs some sleep." "Yes, and I need to know what time to open the Ice Cream Parlour," said Miss Pink Cat.

"The farm rooster always knows when it's morning," said Tessie Bear. Noddy agreed and built a little house in the Town Square for the rooster. "Please cock-a-doodle-doo when the sun rises, so we know it's time to get up," Noddy told him.

"Now we'll know when to get up," said Big-Ears, "but we need to know the time during the day. Let's make a sundial." He made a clock face on the ground and placed a stick in its centre. The shadow of the stick fell across the clock at the right time!

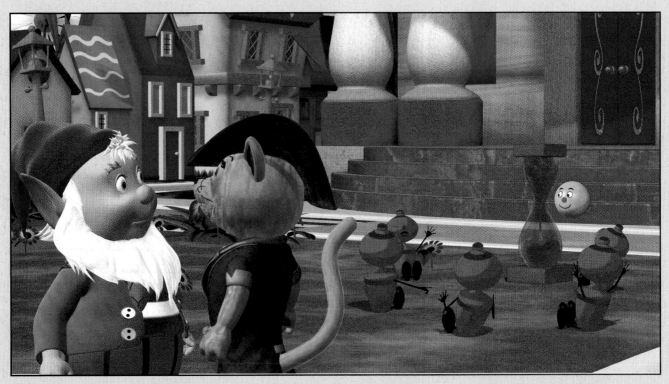

"We'll know when it's morning and we can see the hours passing," said Big-Ears. "We just need a way of counting the minutes." "We can use my egg timer," said Miss Pink Cat. "The Skittle children can flip it over when the sand has trickled through."

When Mr Sparks came back, everyone told him what had happened. "Oh, dear," he said. "I'd better wind all the clocks so you can get back to normal." Noddy explained that they had made clocks of their own: the rooster, the sundial and the egg timer!

Mr Sparks went to the Town Hall and wound up the clock, before checking the time on his watch and putting it right. Noddy was pleased to hear the chimes again. "That's better!" he sighed, before going to sleep. "One clock is better than three!"

WHAT TIME IS IT?

Noddy can have a normal day now that the clocks are right again! Look at these times in Noddy's day and draw the small hand on each clock so that it tells the right time.

Noddy leaves his House-For-One at 9 o'clock.

Noddy goes out for lunch with Tessie Bear at 1 o'clock.

Noddy goes to Toy Town garage at 3 o'clock.

Big-Ears comes for tea at 5 o'clock.

MR SPARKS' TOOLS

Mr Sparks doesn't mend just the clocks in Toy Town, he mends everything else, too! Look at some of the tools from his toolbox and use a pencil to match each one to its shadow.

HELLO, NODDY AND FRIENDS!

Noddy and his Toy Town friends are saying hello! Look carefully at the picture and see if you can spot the small things shown. Tick off each one as you find it.

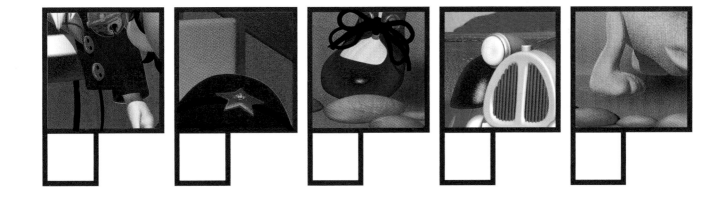

THE BIG RACE

Noddy was having a busy morning. He was rushing to Toy Town Station to collect a passenger, when Mr Plod stopped him. "Noddy, you are driving much too quickly," he said sternly. "The road is not a race track." "I'm sorry," said Noddy. "I shall be more careful."

Noddy had just driven off when Mr Plod felt a sharp push from behind. "Oops!" giggled Martha Monkey. "Sorry, Mr Plod! I couldn't stop in time." "The road through Toy Town is not a race track," Mr Plod told her. "Please roller skate slowly."

As Martha Monkey skated carefully away, Mr Plod was startled by a bell. It was Big-Ears on his bicycle. "Sorry, Mr Plod," he said. "I'm in a hurry." "Everyone is in a hurry today," boomed Mr Plod. "Please slow down, this is not a race track!"

Mr Plod was fed up of telling everyone to slow down. He gathered them together to make an announcement. "Tomorrow there will be a big race from the Town Square," he said. "For just one day, you can speed round the town however you like."

Everyone was very excited indeed about The Big Race and got busy straight away: cars were polished, engines were checked, bicycles were oiled and roller skates were cleaned. They were looking forward to going fast without Mr Plod telling them off!

The next day, Noddy and his friends lined up at the start. "To make it fair, those of you in cars and trucks will have a longer race than the others," Mr Plod explained. "I'll be watching you from Noddy's aeroplane. On your marks, get set…GO!"

Noddy immediately raced ahead of the others. "I'm winning!" he cried, waving to the cheering crowd. Taking his hand off the wheel made Noddy lose control and the car skidded into the pond with a SPLASH! "Oh, no!" said Noddy sadly. "Now I've lost!"

Poor Noddy! With a BRRM! BRRM! Mr Sparks went into the lead in his tow truck, closely followed by Dinah Doll in the fire engine. Big-Ears and Mr Jumbo were not far behind on their bicycles, but Martha Monkey was getting tired on her skates.

The Bouncing Balls were watching the race and started to bounce in all directions when Mr Sparks and Dinah Doll sped towards them. Ding-a-ling-a-ling! Dinah Doll rang the fire bell but the balls bounced even more so that both trucks had to stop.

Big-Ears and Mr Jumbo were pedalling hard on their bicycles past the farm. "Come on, Mr Jumbo!" called Big-Ears, but Mr Jumbo was not used to so much exercise and he was getting tired. He got left behind as Big-Ears cycled off…the wrong way!

Master Tubby Bear had chosen to race on a horse and had taken a short cut. When the Skittle children saw him coming, they giggled so much that they began to fall over and roll around in the road. "Whoah!" cried Master Tubby Bear, stopping his horse.

Martha Monkey was still making an effort at the back of the race, but the naughty goblins had decided to join in. As they wildly pedalled their rickshaw to catch up with the others, they clattered past Martha, startling her and making her tumble over.

Mr Plod saw Sly and Gobbo from Noddy's aeroplane, high above Toy Town, and decided they would be out of the race for knocking someone over. "Is there anyone else left?" he wondered. Noddy and his friends seemed to have stopped or got lost!

Mr Plod was surprised to see Clockwork Mouse in the race…floating along with a bunch of balloons! He had been watching the others and holding the balloons when a gust of wind blew him upwards. "Hold on!" Mr Plod called. "You could win!"

Mr Plod was right: everyone cheered as Clockwork Mouse finished first. "You all had an exciting time," said Mr Plod, "but you've learnt how careful you must be when travelling quickly. So from now on, remember – the road is not a race track!"

BIG-EARS' BICYCLE

Big-Ears enjoyed cycling in The Big Race, even if he did get a little lost! Can you remember what his bicycle looks like? Use a pencil to match Big-Ears to his bicycle and then do the same for Noddy and Mr Plod.

NAUGHTY SLY

There once was a goblin called Sly,
Who stole a plane so he could fly.
"Oh, Noddy won't mind,
He's ever so kind!"
He said as he zoomed round the sky.

BIG RACE BALLOONS

Everyone cheered when Clockwork Mouse crossed the finish line holding on to his bunch of balloons. Now he has let them go, count how many there are of each colour and write the numbers in the boxes below. Be quick, before they float away!

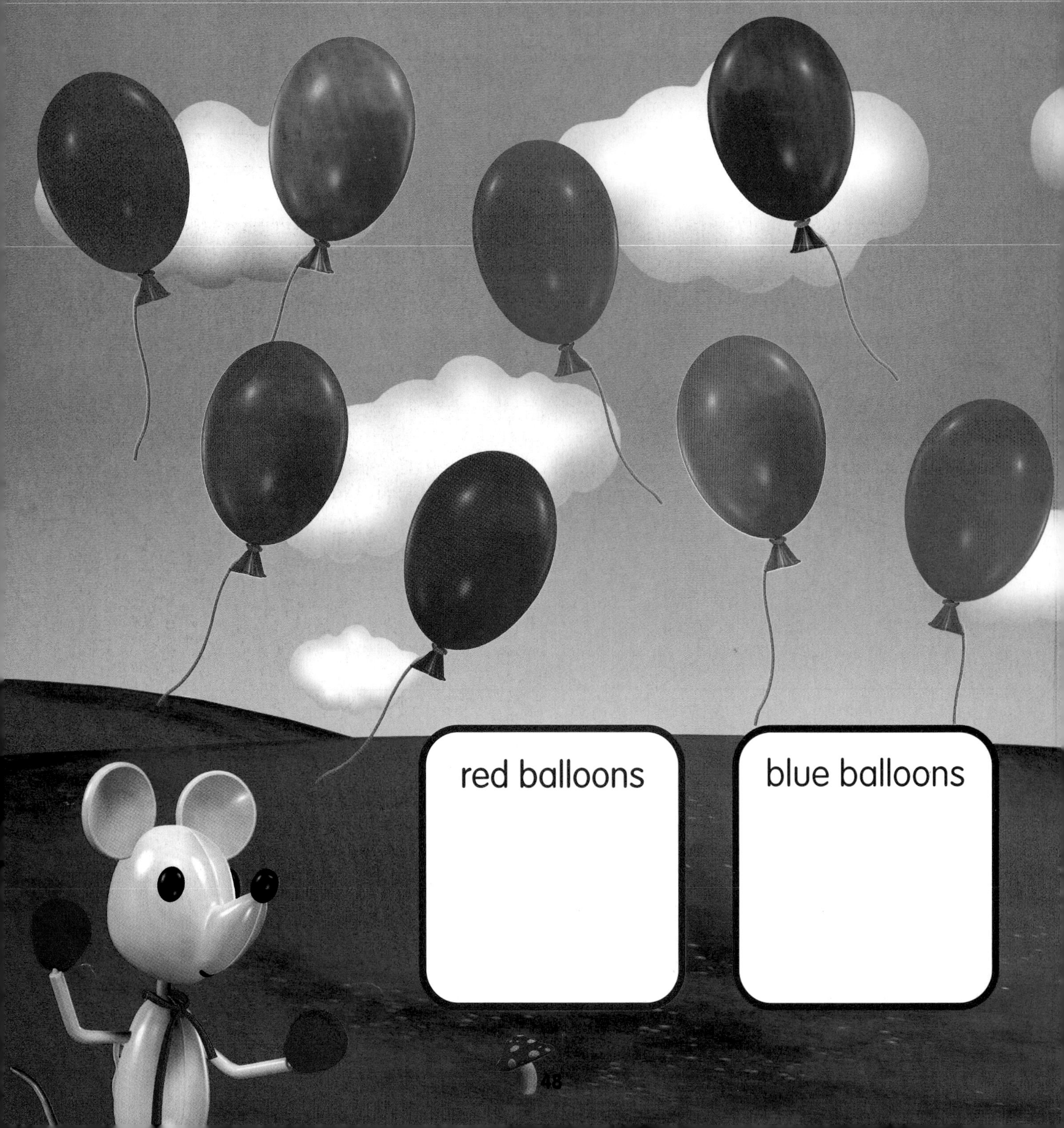

red balloons

blue balloons

yellow balloons

pink balloons

green balloons

49

NOT BEDTIME YET

My eyes feel really tired,
My legs are aching, too.
I should get in my bed soon,
I do know that, I do!

It's just my mind's not tired
Inside my nodding head,
That's why I need a story
Before I go to bed!

Use your pens or
pencils to give Noddy
some colourful pyjamas
to sleep in!

NODDY'S BEDTIME STORIES

Noddy and the Photograph

Noddy and the Magic Muffins

Noddy and the Missing Football

NODDY AND THE PHOTOGRAPH

Noddy loved to take photographs and he had a special new camera: it could be set to take pictures all on its own. One afternoon, he decided he would use it to take a photograph of himself with all his friends and asked Big-Ears to help him.

"That sounds marvellous, Noddy," said Big-Ears. "I'll set up the camera outside the Town Hall and find some blocks for everyone to stand on."

Noddy set off in his taxi to gather his friends for their picture and decided to pick up Tessie Bear first, but she didn't want to come straight away.

"I need time to choose which bonnet to wear," she said. "Do you think pink looks nice in a photo, or green?"

"I'll come back when you've decided," Noddy smiled.

Noddy fetched Mrs Skittle with one of her children and Tiny Ball. He took them to the Town Hall, but Tiny Ball kept rolling off his block and the little Skittle just wanted to play!

"Oh, dear," thought Noddy. "I hope they will stay still long enough to be photographed. This isn't going to be as easy as I thought!"

Things got even trickier. Mr Wobbly Man kept wobbling about, so Martha Monkey wouldn't stand next to him because she said he made her feel seasick.

"I am good at standing still, even when the train is rocking," said the Train Conductor, helpfully. "I'll stand by Mr Wobbly Man."

But each time the train approached, the Conductor had to run back to the station to do his job.

"Oh, dear," sighed Noddy. "I shall have to take the picture when there isn't a trainin the station."

54

Miss Pink Cat
arrived late, as she
had mislaid her
hat. That reminded
Noddy to go back for
Tessie Bear, who had
decided to wear her pink bonnet.
On the way to the Town Hall, he told her that he was worried about
everyone staying still for the photograph.
"Bumpy Dog will keep them in place," said Tessie Bear. "He rounds up the
chickens and chickens never go where you want them to."
Bumpy Dog rounded up Clockwork Clown, Clockwork Mouse, Mr Jumbo
and Mr Sparks, barking as he chased them into place.
"Once my spring has run down I shall stay very still, Noddy," said Clockwork
Clown, "I promise."
Clockwork Mouse promised to stay still too. Mr Jumbo needed two blocks
because he was so big, so Clockwork Mouse shared his block.

"The sun will be setting soon, Noddy," Big-Ears warned. "You need to hurry if you are to take your picture today."

"Master Tubby Bear," called Noddy, as he raced down the street in his taxi. "Come and take your place for the photo, quickly!"

"Halt, in the name of Plod," boomed Mr Plod. "You are driving too fast, young Noddy."

"Sorry, Mr Plod," gasped Noddy. "I'm trying to photograph everyone and Big-Ears says the sun is going down and we have to be quick and –"

"Toot!" went Mr Plod's whistle. "Calm down, Noddy. A photo, you say? Well, that calls for my best uniform…"

The two naughty goblins never miss anything and had heard about the photograph.

"Can we be in your picture, Noddy? Please," whined Gobbo.
"We handsome goblins will make your photo look better," added Sly.
Noddy agreed to let the goblins be in the picture as long as they were next to Mr Plod, so he could keep an eye on them.
At last, it seemed that everyone was in position.
"Oh, no!" cried Noddy. "I thought I had found everyone but the block at the front is empty. Who is missing, Big-Ears?"
"Silly Noddy," laughed Big-Ears. "It's you!"
Noddy set the camera and ran to his block.
"Smile everyone!" he exclaimed.
Click! What a lovely photograph!

'Click!'

NODDY AND THE MAGIC MUFFINS

Wise old gnome Big-Ears was very good at magic and would sometimes teach Noddy his tricks. Noddy was looking through the spell book one afternoon when he spotted a recipe for magic muffins.

"Magic muffins?" he chuckled. "What are they, Big-Ears?"

"Well, they're very special muffins," Big-Ears replied. "You take one bite and ask for something, then the muffin changes into what you've asked for. Would you like to make some?"

"Ooh, yes please," smiled Noddy. "But what happens if you take more than one bite?"

"Then the spell will go wrong," said Big-Ears.

Noddy helped
Big-Ears to make
the special muffins
and they put them
in the oven. The
smell as they
baked was
delicious!
"They certainly
smell magical," said
Noddy, breathing in the
sweet aroma. The smell
wafted through Toadstool Wood and into the
Dark Wood, bringing the goblins running. They spied
on Noddy and Big-Ears through their telescope.
"Mmm, muffins," drooled Sly. "My favourite!"
"Mine too," Gobbo agreed. "We just need to
work out a way of stealing some!"
Once the muffins were ready, Noddy
took them out of the oven and Big-
Ears told him to leave them by the
open window to cool.

When the muffins were cool enough, Big-Ears took one
from the plate. To show Noddy what to do, he took a bite
and put the muffin on the table before saying his spell:
In my hands I'd like to hold
Many glittering coins of gold!
Noddy squealed with delight as a shower of magic
sparkles turned the muffin into a pot full of gold.
"They're magic muffins!" hissed Gobbo outside, peering
down the telescope. "Even better!"
"Let me see!" said Sly excitedly, grabbing the telescope.
He watched as Noddy took a bite from his muffin and placed
it in front him on the table.

Noddy thought of his spell and ran to get a spoon before he said it aloud:
 What I'd really love, of course,
   Is lots of ice cream…with cherries and sauce!
   Noddy watched with amazement as his muffin turned into the biggest
   dish of ice cream he had ever seen. He dug his spoon in and tasted
   some: it was delicious!
   "I can't eat all this myself, Big-Ears," he smiled. "You will have to help me!"
   While Noddy and Big-Ears were eating their ice cream, Gobbo crept up
   to the window and snatched a muffin. Before he could get a second
   one, Big-Ears spotted him and shouted, "Hey!"

"Quick! Let's do a spell," said Gobbo, running away. "Noddy and Big-Ears had to eat some muffin first, so…"

Gobbo took a bite from the muffin. It was so nice that he took another.

"That's lovely!" he said, spraying crumbs everywhere. "Now, let's have a new bike."

Gobbo put the muffin on the floor and said:

This little muffin is not what it seems,

Make it a bike that's so new, it gleams!

Noddy caught up with the goblins and watched as the magic sparkles turned the muffin into a bike. It wasn't shiny and new, though; it was old and twisted!

"It's gone wrong!" wailed Gobbo. "Please tell us how to change it, Noddy!"

Noddy knew why the spell had gone wrong, but he wouldn't tell the goblins.

"But it has a wheel missing," said Sly. "It's no use!"

"Well, that will teach you not to mess around with magic," Noddy told him, sternly.

Noddy went back to Toadstool House and told Big-Ears what had happened. Then his little bell began to jingle as he had an idea.

"Big-Ears, seeing that broken old bike has made me think how nice our bikes are," he said. "Let's go for a ride through the countryside."

"I can't think of a better way to spend an afternoon," agreed Big-Ears. "Now we can have a different kind of magical day!"

NODDY AND THE MISSING FOOTBALL

When Sly and Gobbo had nothing to do, they would end up doing something naughty. They had nothing to do most days.

"I know," said Gobbo. "Let's have a game of football!"

"Yes!" agreed Sly excitedly, jumping up and doing some warm-up exercises. "I love football!"

Sly stopped when he realised that something was missing.

"How will we play football without a ball?" he asked.

"We steal one from Noddy, silly!" sneered Gobbo. "Come on."

The two naughty goblins crept through the Dark Wood towards Noddy's House-For-One in Toy Town.

That morning, Noddy was about to play football with his friends and was having a practice outside first. He put the football in his car while he went back inside to check he had left his little house tidy.

"Could that be any easier?" giggled Gobbo, watching from behind a nearby bush. "Go on!" He pushed Sly towards Noddy's car. Panicking, Sly snatched the ball and dashed back behind the bush, just as Noddy came out again.

"Oh, no!" cried Noddy, seeing that the ball was gone. He couldn't see anyone, but he knew who had taken it.

"Sly! Gobbo!" he called crossly. "Bring my ball back at once!"

The goblins only sniggered silently. Eventually, Noddy got fed up of waiting and went to the Police Station to report his missing ball. Tessie Bear saw him driving sadly along later and called out to him to stop.

"Noddy, whatever's the matter?" she asked.

"I was supposed to be playing football," he explained, "but the naughty goblins took my ball. I've been to tell Mr Plod, but he's not there. I shall just have to find something else to do."

Tessie Bear didn't like to see her friend looking so glum. She decided to see if anyone would help her to get the missing football back.

Tessie Bear went to Miss Pink Cat's Ice Cream Parlour and told those there what had happened. She asked if anyone would go to the Dark Wood with her to get Noddy's ball back, but nobody offered.

"What about you, Mr Sparks?" she asked.

"I'm, um, busy," stammered Mr Sparks. "I must get back to the garage."

Tessie Bear asked Mr Wobbly Man, but he said he was too full of ice cream to go anywhere. She asked Martha Monkey, too, but she had to do some roller skating practice. The only person who was happy to help was Clockwork Mouse.

"I know I'm small," he said, "but I can still help."

Tessie Bear, Bumpy Dog and Clockwork Mouse
made their way to the Dark Wood. It was very
gloomy there.

"What should we do now?" Tessie Bear asked
uncertainly. Clockwork Mouse wasn't quite
sure of what to do either.

"Look!" he said suddenly, pointing. "A toadstool
has been broken over there. The goblins
probably did it while they were playing with
Noddy's football."

Clockwork Mouse was right. Sly and Gobbo,
who were listening from a hiding place nearby,
fidgeted and rustled.

"Woof! Woof!" barked Bumpy Dog, hearing
the goblins and bounding towards them.

"All right!" cried Gobbo. "You can
have the ball back!"

Clockwork Mouse grabbed the football and took it back to Toy Town with Tessie Bear and Bumpy Dog. Mr Plod was back, so they told him what had happened and he put the naughty goblins in his jail for stealing.

"Thank you Tessie," said Noddy, "and thank you, Clockwork Mouse. Now we can all have that game of football!" Noddy thanked Bumpy Dog, too, by giving him a juicy bone as a reward for sniffing out the goblins.

Noddy's friends were so proud of Clockwork Mouse that they lifted him up and gave him three cheers. He was, after all, the bravest little mouse in Toy Town!

PHOTO STORY

Can you remember what happened in the Noddy and the Photograph story? Look at these pictures and put them in the right order, then retell the story in your own words. The answer is at the bottom of the page.

A

B

C

D

Answer: d, b, c, a.

FOOTBALL FUN

Noddy was very pleased indeed to get his ball back from the naughty goblins. Now Bumpy Dog wants to join in the fun, too! Use your crayons or pencils to colour this picture of Noddy playing football with Bumpy Dog.

MUFFIN DAY IN TOY TOWN

Look at all these googleberry muffins that Dinah Doll has baked for Muffin Day! Noddy loves sweet treats and thinks they look delicious. There are ten other sweet treats hidden around the picture – see if you can spot them all!

B IS FOR BIG-EARS

Noddy's best friend's name begins with the 'b' sound: Big-Ears. Use a pencil to practise writing the letters in these other words that begin with the 'b' sound.

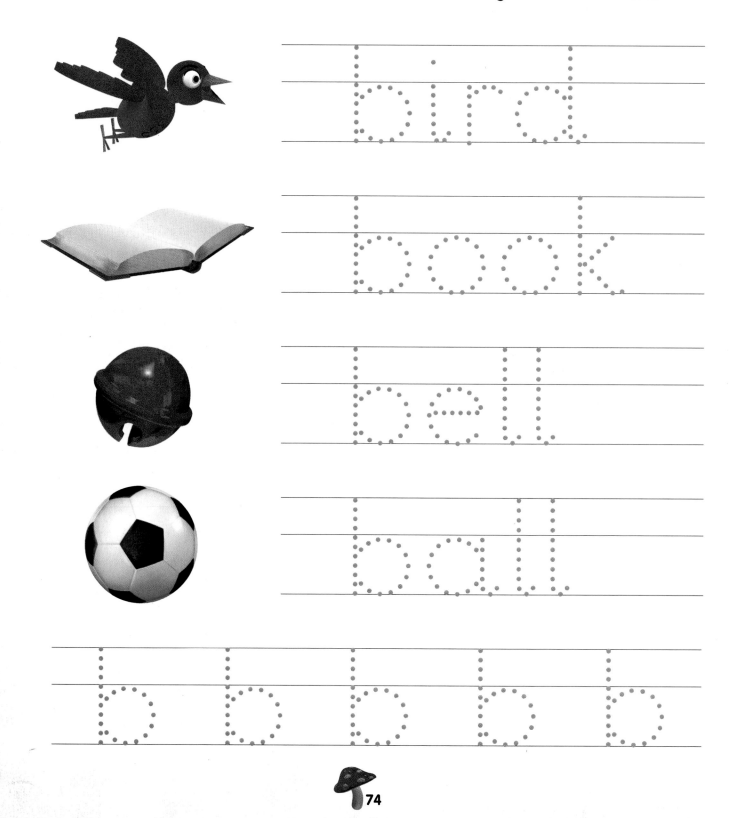

bird

book

bell

ball

b b b b

WHO AM I?

See if you can guess who this Toy Town favourite is from his little rhyme!
The answer is at the bottom of the page.

I wibble wobble this way and that,
I always wear a pink top hat.
My shirt is white, my jacket's blue,
I wear a colourful waistcoat, too!
I have a green and yellow bow tie,
I'm Noddy's friend – who am I?

Answer: I'm Mr Wobbly Man!

THE TOY TOWN TREASURE HUNT

Dinah Doll went to see Noddy one morning, as she was worried about Big-Ears. "He was supposed to come and choose prizes for the treasure hunt last night, but he didn't arrive," she explained. "I'll go to Toadstool House and see if he's all right," smiled Noddy.

76

Noddy drove through Toadstool Wood until he got to Big-Ears' house. "Hello!" he called. "Big-Ears!" There was no reply, so Noddy went inside to see if his friend was there. As he saw no sign of him in the living room, Noddy went to look upstairs.

Noddy noticed some sheets of paper on the table. He read the top sheet, which said: Travel there and smoothly back, in an engine on a track, You must buy a ticket too, that is where you'll find a clue. "Big-Ears must be hiding clues," Noddy said aloud.

Noddy soon solved the clue and rushed to Toy Town Station to buy a ticket from the conductor. On it was written: Time to leave the railway track, stop by for an ice cream snack, Miss Pink Cat will welcome you and help you find the third clue.

Noddy got back in his car and drove to Miss Pink Cat's Ice Cream Parlour. "I hope Big-Ears is still here," he said to himself. "Dinah Doll is waiting for news." Big-Ears was nowhere to be seen, so Noddy asked Miss Pink Cat if she could help.

"Big-Ears wrote something on one of my menus," said Miss Pink Cat. "Here it is."
Noddy read the next clue: Vanilla cream and toffee ice are not for sale where you
must go, In a place where cars are fixed is a person who will know.

Noddy guessed that his next stop would be the garage and hoped that he would
catch up with Big-Ears there. He didn't find him, but Mr Sparks was waiting with
a note that had been hidden in his toolbox. "See what it says, Noddy," he smiled.

Noddy looked at the fourth clue: The round part of a hammer head is the part that knocks, A round shape in the old Town Hall is one that ticks and tocks. "The Town Hall clock is round," said Noddy. "And it ticks and tocks! I shall go there next."

Noddy went to the Town Hall and looked up at the clock. It chimed ten o'clock and on the tenth chime, a piece of paper fluttered out! It said: Tick-tock, tick-tock, I always show the time, Mr Plod will help you with the clue that solves the crime.

Noddy went to see Mr Plod and told him that he was looking for Big-Ears, but could find only clues. "Don't worry, little Noddy," said Mr Plod. "I'm sure you'll catch up with Big-Ears soon. Come with me and I'll show you where the next clue is."

Mr Plod took Noddy into the Police Station and pointed to a 'Wanted' poster for a naughty goblin thief. At the bottom, it said: I know I have been naughty and I know you'll hunt for me, I'm sitting in a hollow underneath a Dark Wood tree.

"Oh, dear," thought Noddy. He didn't like going to the Dark Wood, but he wanted to find Big-Ears. He drove there quickly, but Big-Ears had gone and there didn't seem to be another clue. What Noddy didn't know was that the goblins had found it.

"You're good at puzzles, Sly," said Gobbo. "Solve this and we can pretend we've solved them all!" Sly read the clue: If you can read things back to front, inside out and upside down, Claim your prize at s'haniD llats in the centre of the town.

Sly worked out that the two strange words said Dinah's stall backwards. "Let's go and get our prize!" he grinned. The goblins pushed to the front of the queue and asked for the prize, but Big-Ears had just arrived. He knew that they must have cheated!

Noddy was pleased to see his friend. "I followed the clues, but couldn't find the last one," he explained. "The goblins took it," said Big-Ears. "You can have a prize for solving them all, then we shall write more clues for another treasure hunt tomorrow!"

CLEVER CLUES

Big-Ears has decided to do a different sort of treasure hunt by giving Noddy and each of his friends a clue to an everyday object. They have to solve the clue and take their object to Big-Ears. Help Noddy and his friends to solve the clues and draw your own picture of what each one has to find! The answers are at the bottom of the page.

What must Noddy find? Draw it here!

This fruit with thick skin is curved and yellow,
If there's one in your bowl, you're a lucky fellow!

What must Tessie Bear find? Draw it here!

This has a handle, a lid and a spout,
You lift it and tip it to pour your tea out.

What must Master Tubby Bear find? Draw it here!

You might play outside with this toy that is round,
You kick it and catch it and bounce it around.

What must Martha Monkey find? Draw it here!

This stick's made of wax and need it you might
If you're stuck in the dark – burn it and there's light.

What must Clockwork Mouse find? Draw it here!

These green things grow on a flower or tree,
Find one that's fallen and bring it to me.

Answers: Noddy must find a banana, Tessie Bear must find a teapot,
Master Tubby Bear must find a ball, Martha Monkey must find a candle,
Clockwork Mouse must find a leaf.

TREASURE AND TREATS

Everyone in Toy Town loves to do a treasure hunt so they can win a treat! Treasure and treat begin with the 'tr' sound, which is made by 't' and 'r' together. Use a pencil to practise writing the 'tr' sound in these words.

_ _ _ e e   _ _ i a n g l e

_ _ _ u c k s   _ _ a i n

PERFECT PRIZES

Everyone who solved Big-Ears' clues got to choose a prize from Dinah Doll's stall. Follow the strings from Master Tubby Bear, Martha Monkey and Tessie Bear to find out which prize each one chose. The answers are at the bottom of the page.

Answers: Master Tubby Bear chose a football, Martha Monkey chose a yo-yo and Tessie Bear chose a flower.

NODDY'S BOAT RACE

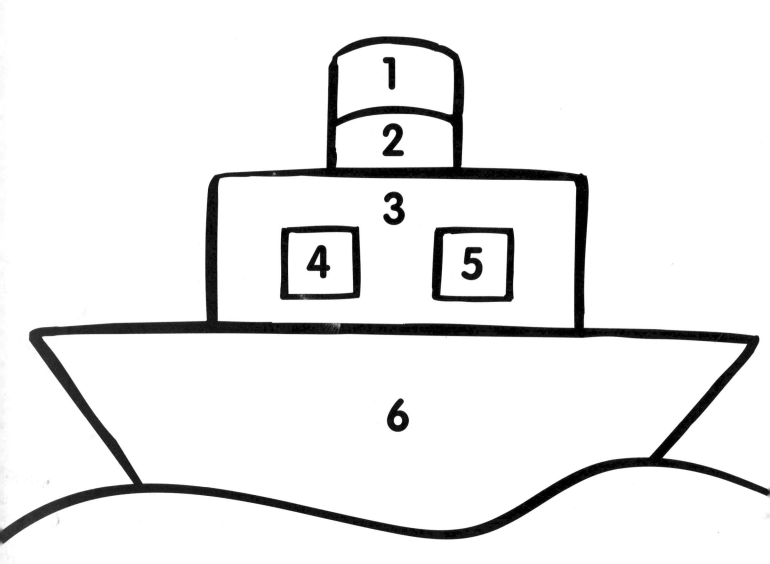

Noddy loves to play with his boat at the pond in Toy Town! You and a friend can use these boats to play a fun colouring game. All you need are some crayons or pens and a dice. Take turns to throw the dice and colour in the part marked with the number shown on the dice. If you have already coloured that part, you must wait until your next turn to try again. The first one to colour all six parts of their boat is the winner!

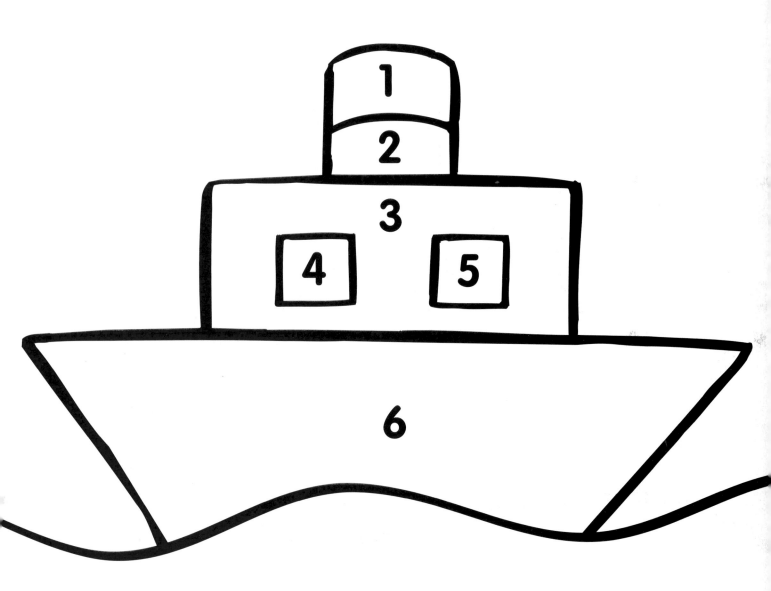

THE MIXED-UP PAINT TINS

It was very late at night in Toy Town. Everyone was fast asleep in bed… except for Sly and Gobbo, the naughty goblins. They were wide awake! They crept through the dark, quiet streets to Mr Sparks' garage and, making sure no one was looking, went inside.

Gobbo smiled when he saw all the exciting things lying around in the garage. He went over to a row of tins on the floor. Their lids were all different colours: yellow, red, purple, blue, green and orange. "Do you know what's in these tins, Sly?" he asked.

Sly licked his lips. "Jam?" he replied, hopefully. "Or sticky syrup?" Gobbo reminded him that they were in a garage. "It's paint, silly," he told him. The goblins took the paint lids off, one by one. "Oh, good," said Gobbo. "Red's my favourite colour."

Sly scooped out some blue paint and rubbed it on his hands. "Look!" he giggled, leaving blue handprints all over the garage wall. "I can make a pretty pattern!" "So can I!" Gobbo cackled, dipping his feet in the red paint and walking around.

The goblins were having so much fun that they didn't notice the sun coming up and were surprised to hear the rooster's morning 'Cock-a-doodle-doo!' They quickly put the lids on the paint pots before tiptoeing out of the garage and scurrying away.

The goblins escaped just in time – Mr Sparks had a busy day ahead and came to open the garage early. Master Tubby Bear arrived soon afterwards, as he had agreed to help repaint Noddy's car. "I'll show you where the paints are," said Mr Sparks.

Mr Sparks took Master Tubby Bear into the garage and showed him the paint pots with the red and yellow lids. "As you know, Noddy's car is red and yellow," he said, "so you will need these two tins of paint. I'll see if I can find you an apron."

Just then, there was a 'Parp! Parp!' outside the garage as Noddy drove up. "Hello, Noddy," called Mr Sparks, coming out to greet him. "We're all ready to repaint your car and make it as good as new." "Thank you, Mr Sparks," smiled Noddy.

It was only then that Mr Sparks noticed the mess on his walls. "Handprints!" he gasped. "This must have something to do with the goblins. I shall let Mr Plod know." If only Mr Sparks knew that the goblins had also mixed up the lids on his paint tins!

Master Tubby Bear got to work. "This is a funny yellow," he said, frowning at the orange paint. "And this red paint looks more like purple to me, but Mr Sparks must know his colours." The young bear painted all morning to get his job done.

At last Master Tubby Bear had finished. Noddy's car was bright and sparkling… but it didn't look quite the same as Master Tubby Bear remembered it. Even the little car itself was unhappy and gave a sad 'Parp!' Noddy arrived and cried out in alarm.

"Master Tubby Bear!" he gasped. "What have you done to my car?" Noddy's shouts brought everyone running to look. "What strange colours," said Martha Monkey. "They're pretty," added Tessie Bear, "but it doesn't look like Noddy's car."

"Why did you change the colours, Master Tubby Bear?" Mr Sparks asked sternly. Luckily, wise Big-Ears had arrived. "Master Tubby Bear is not to blame," he said, peering at the tins. "The colours on these lids don't match the paint in the tins."

Mr Sparks called Mr Plod, who soon solved The Case of the Mixed-Up Paint Tins. Realising at once whose feet had left the red footprints, he followed them out of the garage to the tree where the goblins were hiding and arrested them at once.

Mr Plod marched Sly and Gobbo back to the garage. "Now, you two naughty goblins can scrub away your blue handprints and red footprints," he boomed. "Then you will paint Noddy's purple and orange car its proper colours again: red and yellow!"

TOY TOWN COLOURS

Mr Plod is checking that the goblins haven't changed the colour of anything else in Toy Town! Say what colour each of these Toy Town things is and then use a pencil to draw a circle round the odd one out in each row.

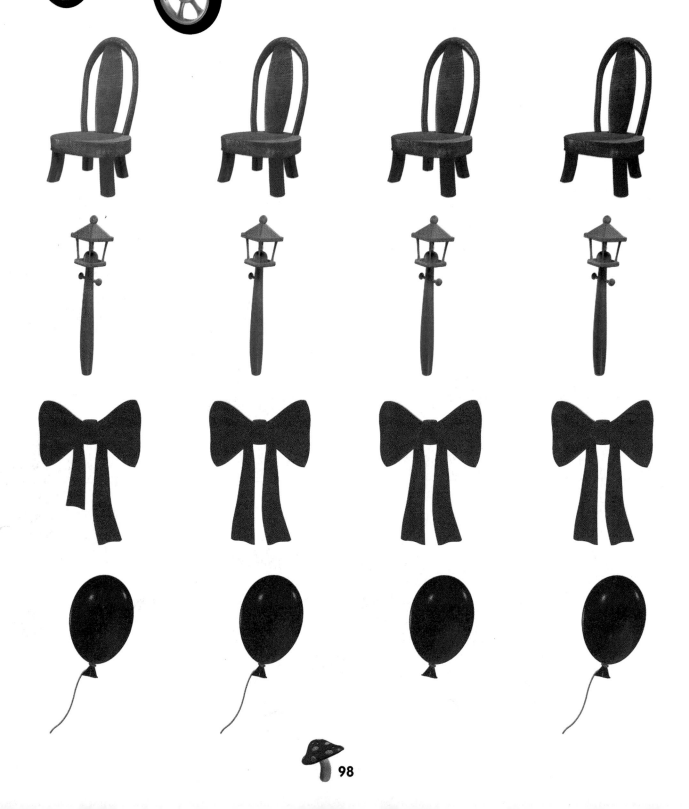

RED AND YELLOW FELLOW

Noddy's little car just wasn't the same when it was purple and orange! Lots of Noddy's belongings are red and yellow. Look at the red and yellow items here and use a pencil to match up the pairs. Then draw a circle round the one left over.

THINGS THAT GO TOGETHER

Master Tubby Bear is making sure he has the right paint for his next job! To paint something, he needs a paintbrush and a paint pot. Use a pencil to match up the other things that go together on this page.

GIVE THE DOG
A BONE

Bumpy Dog had a juicy bone earlier and now he can't remember where he left it!
Use a pencil or your finger to show Bumpy which way to go to get his bone back.

BLESS YOU, MR. JUMBO!

Join in this story by saying what the pictures are as they appear.

Noddy

Kite

Martha Monkey

Mr. Jumbo

Whenever  had any spare time in between taking passengers around

Toy Town, he would go and fly his  . He was trying to fly it one day, when

 stopped to watch. ran with the and threw it up into the air,

but it fell straight back down. laughed as ran with it again

and still had no luck. "You may as well give up!" she chuckled. didn't want to

give up just yet. He knew that if he could just get his up far enough to catch the wind, it would fly perfectly.  was out for his walk and he also stopped to see

what was doing. As he watched, he felt a tickle in his trunk. "Oh, dear,"

said . "Oh, no!" exclaimed , seeing that he was about to sneeze.

Everyone in Toy Town knew that they had to get out of the way if sneezed.

"Ah…aah…" began . "Ah..AAAATCHOOO!" He did a great big Jumbo sneeze

and sent a strong gust of air towards Noddy's . "Hooray!" cheered ,

holding on to the string as his flew way up into the sky and bobbed

about on the breeze up there. "I knew I would get to fly my if I kept on trying!

Bless you, …and thanks!"

GET DOWN, BUMPY DOG!

Bumpy Dog is always jumping up at Noddy. Get down, Bumpy Dog! Look carefully at the two pictures and see if you spot the five differences in the second one. The answers are at the bottom of the page.

Answers: 1. The butterfly has moved. 2. Big-Ears has moved. 3. A flower has appeared. 4. A bird has appeared. 5. Noddy's bell is missing.

104

IMPORTANT PEOPLE

People are very important, so their names always begin with a capital letter.
Use a pencil to write the capital letters in the names of Noddy and his friends
and then add your name too!

__oddy

__ig-Ears

__r __lod

__iss __ink __at

My Name is:

A WALK
IN THE RAIN

It takes more than a little shower to stop Noddy and Tessie Bear going for their stroll. Besides, it's nice to walk in the rain and share an umbrella with a friend! Use your crayons or pens to colour this picture, copying the colours from the opposite page.

TIME FOR AN ICE CREAM!

1 START HERE

2

3

13

14

15

16 You find a lucky coin! Play again.

17

18

19

20

21 Miss a go while you ask Big-Ears if he would like an ice cream too.

Noddy is having a break between passengers and would like to go for a Googleberry Surprise at Miss Pink Cat's Ice Cream Parlour! Find a dice and counters so that you and a friend or two can drive through Toy Town with Noddy to get a delicious ice cream. Choose a counter for each player and place the counters on the start. Take turns to throw the dice and work your way round Toy Town, making sure you throw a six to start. The first one to reach the Ice Cream Parlour is the winner!

4

5

6 You spot a balloon! Run on two spaces to catch it.

7

8

12

11 Mrs Skittle says hello. Miss a go to chat with her.

10

9

22

23

24

25